SUCCESS
Is An Attitude

———————— Title of Book ————————

"SUCCESS IS AN ATTITUDE!"

Bo,
Success is yours!
You are my barber and
you are always positive,
Keep working hard and thinking big,
It will pay off soon.

Sincerely

"Mr. Motivator"

SUCCESS
Is An Attitude

——————————Title of Book—————————

"SUCCESS IS AN ATTITUDE!"

THAT CAN LEAD YOU TO THE DISCOVERY OF YOUR
DESIGN OR PURPOSE IN LIFE.

Dwight Jeffery

Order this book online at www.trafford.com
or email orders@trafford.com

Most Trafford titles are also available at major online book retailers.

Printed in the United States of America.

ISBN: 978-1-4269-5401-6 (sc)
ISBN: 978-1-4269-5412-2 (e)

Library of Congress Control Number: 2011900568

Trafford rev. 01/31/2011

 www.trafford.com

North America & international
toll-free: 1 888 232 4444 (USA & Canada)
phone: 250 383 6864 ✦ fax: 812 355 4082

Acknowledgments

I would like to thank all of the people that contributed to my life by using their talents and abilities to inspire me to be who I am today. Each of us have something within us that can make a difference in someone's life. Please, forgive me if I've missed some dear people, but I tried my best to honor everyone that I could remember.

Martin Luther King, Jr., Mahatma Gandhi, John F. Kennedy, George Bush, Bill Clinton, John Kennedy, Jr., President Barack Obama, Robert E. Price, Frederick K.C. Price, Joel Osteen, T.D. Jakes, Ronald Jones, Robert Turner, Arthur James Mooring, Billy W. Craig, David L. Venters, James Turknett, Alonzo Johnson, Jr., Bill Winston, Creflo Dollar, Billy Graham, Cesar Oviedo, Regis Perkins, Wardell Clark, Jeffery Brown, Avery Jones, John Ruth, Jonathan Reagor, Frederick Haynes, Thomas Smith, David Davidson, Rickey Rush, Max Robinson, Peter Jennings, Walter Cronkite, Tom Brokaw, Tracey Rowlett, Troy Dungan, John McCaa, Jeff Crilley, Ozzie Davis, Richard Pryor, Eddie Murphy, Bernie Mac, Steve Harvey, Cedric the Entertainer, Tom Joyner, Rickey Smiley, Tyler Perry, George Lopez, Charlie Murphy, Rodney Dangerfield, Jamie Fox, Jay Lamont, Redd Foxx, George Wallace, Louie Anderson, George Carland, Don Rickles, Tim Conway, Harvey Korman, Johnny Carson, Will Smith, Earl Graves, John H. Johnson, Earvin "Magic" Johnson, Muhammad Ali, Clint Eastwood, Denzel Washington, Emmanuel Burrell, Roland Jones, Philip Shafen, Jr., Charlie Wright, Roy McClone, B.T. Caldwell, O.Z. Ford, Nig Jeffery, Ralph T. Jeffery, Norris Jeffery, Roy Smith, Louis Smith, Royce Jeffery, Sr., Royce Jeffery, Jr., Rex Smith, Micheal Griffin, Robert L.

Curry, Homer Lee Wright, Theodore Johnson, Tulley Johnson, Ed (Sug) Johnson, Dwight G. Traylor, Cypheen Kabongu, Clevon (Judge) Jones, Glenn Hawkins, Lynn Hawkins, Hoy S. Farr, Travis Farr, Ron Anderson, Glenn Williams, Michael Williams, Reginald Khanard Steward, Manuel L. Weaver, Cecil W. Edwards, Michael Fortson, Carl Bryant, Jr., Pee Wee Moore, Anthony Bowens, Rand Duke, James Gardner, Gary Charles Johnson, Charles Brumell, Pat Turner, Preston Smith, Patrick Beacham, Ralph Mills, Michael Bland, Jeremiah Oliphant, Freddie Simpson, Lonnie VanZandt, LaDarien Spencer, Tom Lacey, Abron Lattiere, Randall Primm, Mark Hansford, Jesse Robertson, Jr., L.C. Goodman, Jake Patterson, Will Jones, Damron Caraway, Troy Johnson, Alex Gonzalez, Eddie Williams, Ed Shields, Raymond Thomas, Allen Brooks, Ken Perry, Abi Martinez, Edward Dee Griffin, Tommy Lee White, James Davis, Grover Washington, Jr., Bobby Robinson, James Beck, J.T. Beck, Irving Smith, Jr., Eddie Joe Smith, Kenny Smith, General Lee Beck, Jerry Beck, Jake Patterson, Sam Dixon, Melvin Steed, Claude Steed, Terry Bryant, Johnny Webb, K.W. Lane, Vernon Washington, Berry Luster, Jeff (Buddy) Carr, Mark Hughey, James Kazee, John Menning, Matthew Menning, Steve Klein, Bill Raley, Ed Hearne, Oliver (Ambitious) Jackson, and G.F. Soldier.

Among the women, individuals such as Coretta Scott King, Mary Kay Ash, Jacqueline Kennedy Onassis, Lena Horne, Eddie Bernice Johnson, Earline D. Jones, Barbara Jordan, Maya Angelou, Margaret Thatcher, Cicely Tyson, Oprah Winfrey, Halle Berry, Jennifer Lopez, Martha Stewart, Barbara Walters, Diahann Carroll, Ruby Dee, CeCe Winans, Candi Staten Sauswell, Patti LaBelle, Gladys Knight, Aretha Franklin, Diana Ross, Beyonce Knowles, Carol Burnett, Monique, Phyllis Diller, Moms Mabley, Lucille Ball, Mary Tyler Moore, Diane Ragsdale, Annie Dickson, Joanne Robertson, Dr. Lorene B. Holmes, Nikki Hunter, Linda Hall, Geraldine Hughes, Brenda Brothers, Chandra Carroll, Tiffany Harden, Daylene Carter, Gloria King, Alberta Williams, Clarice Hardiman, Estell Brooks, Mary Sandoval, Lupe Moralez, Adrian Brown, Mozella Brown, Serita Jakes, and First Lady, Michelle Obama. Also, included are the following: Rosetta Canady, Mavis Adams, Ludie Wright, Jerlene Jeffery, Lurline Jeffery, Maggie Curry, Ruthie Wright, Blanche Smith, Emma Lewis Smith, Alice R. Johnson, Alma R. West, Diane Traylor, Louise Beard, Eunice Brinkley, Sharon Jeffery, DeShunna Kabongu, Pauline Jeffery, Thelma Smith, Blanche Smith, Marilyn Sue Starnes, Mary Lane, Eulla Mae Edwards, Delain Easley, Matilda Edwards, Rhonda Craig,

Dorothy Faye Brown, Verna Mae Jones, Elvie Craig, Mary Louise Johnson, Marcella Venters, Melissa Farr, Darla Williams, Michelle Williams, Joyce Spencer, Sharon Lattiere, Carolyn Primm, Saundra Primm, Roxanna Perkins, Loretta Reagor, Carmen Johnson, Anita Robertson, Michelle Burrell, Sharon Ruth, Shirlyn Smith, Christine Mastin Bitter, Joanne Robertson, Mary McKinney, Estelle Brooks, Joanne Robinson, Estelle Patterson, Earnestine Griffin, Eloise Beck, Barbara Mohon, Mae Len Washington, Redd Elder, Alma Luster, Ruby Lee Davis, Mrs. Cobb, Mertle Smith, Arletha Kazee, Beverly Madison, Sherry Boyd, Mary Griffin, Loyce Bullock, Mozella Brown, Denitra Reed, Diane Williams, Linda Elam, Barbara Robinson, Elizabeth Dattamo, Barbara Ford, Ann Roy, Mozelle Moore, Ellen Menning, Sarah Menning, Jeanette Byrd, Dionne Titus, Felicia Hasan, Pamela Marshall, and Selah.

SUCCESS

Is An Attitude

Dedication

I would like to dedicate this book to the memory of Thomas Sanders, a former student who was killed in November 1999.

His goal was to become a lawyer, so that he could make a difference in his community. He was an amazing young man who possessed a great attitude and a kind heart.

May Thomas Sanders rest in peace.

Table of Contents

Chapter 1 –
"Is your attitude, good or bad?"

Basically, everyone has an attitude to some degree, but the question should be centered around what type of attitude do you possess? Your attitude can be positive or negative. For example, let's look at students. A student with a bad attitude is more likely to get into trouble with an instructor than a student who possesses a positive attitude. Your attitude can harness or change your belief system.

In order to help you see more clearly or understand the power behind an attitude, we must think or take a closer look at how our attitudes can affect us. Our attitudes can make or break us.

First of all, what is an attitude? An attitude is your mental position or feelings regarding something that is factual in your life.

Some people let others think for them and allow their attitudes to be shaped by these influences.

Now, if your influences are positive, it could be beneficial, but this could also lead to disaster if your influences are negative. You must take the responsibility to examine your thoughts, feelings, and reactions to situations or circumstances that get our attention.

1

You cannot control your feelings or emotions, but you can control how you choose to react.

Programming your mind with positives can help to transform a negative attitude into a positive attitude.

By simply observing how you view your life will allow you to focus in on the attitude that may be attached to your character. Your attitude often plays a major role in helping you climb the success ladder or keep you hostage to failure or mental roadblocks.

Your life is what you make of it. Your attitude about life determines whether you will go forward or retreat and give up because of circumstances, obstacles, setbacks, disappointments, or rejections.

Life is sometimes very difficult to face. It always has been and always will be, so don't expect everything to be easy and handed to you.

The attitude of a winner is a mindset and consistent work habit that gets results. Attitude is power. Attitude can give you the power to look beyond our past, education, money, circumstances, failures, successes, and beyond what other people think or say or do. Attitude is the most important asset that you can possess. It's more important then appearance, grade point average, talent or skill.

Life is about choices. It's making the right choices. It's making the right choices in life. You must choose each day deciding what kind of attitude you will carry with you into the sunset.

If you want to be a successful leader, you must look close at your disposition because it will attract what you are on the inside.

Chapter 2 –
"Life is about choices"

You can choose good or either bad success. What is success? What does success mean to you? What have you been taught or conditioned to believe about success?

In actuality, I believe that success is simply taking a real look at where you are in life and then putting together a workable strategy that will catapult your efforts into a realm of achievement.

I remember once when I was in my early twenties, I attended a company convention. One of the company's top level executives was speaking. Everyone was amazed and impressed with this man's production level of success. Our division was escorted on stage to meet him and shake hands with him. We were all very excited to meet him. He shook hands with everyone. But, when he got to me, he refused to shake my hand. I was hurt and embarrassed because I felt the rejection and dishonor in front of the entire audience.

I was humiliated and hurt because of the rejection that I felt when this man refused to shake my hand for whatever reason. The more I thought about it, the angrier I became. I realized that I could not allow my life to be consumed with hatred and anger every time I thought about this man and the rejection that made my stomach cramp.

I chose to forgive that man so that I could move forward with my life. Then, I said to myself, "Someday I will be successful and when I get the opportunity to meet people, I am going to give a warm smile and a friendly handshake to everyone that I encounter especially those that are less fortunate than me.

That was the day I became Mr. Motivator to students, friends, family and to those that are down and out. This attitude shift in my life suddenly changed the circumstances around me and made life more enjoyable.

Sometimes, the worse situations can produce the best medicine for your life. Every individual should be treated with respect and dignity because we are all important. All of us are unique in our own special way.

When you dream and visualize it clearly, just add passion, belief, and enthusiasm. Suddenly, your dream will soon become a reality. "Dare to Dream and Dream Big!"

Says "Mr. Motivator"

Chapter 3 –

"You must avoid distractions"

When you develop a positive attitude and begin to move forward in life or show signs of making progress, you may notice things or people getting in your way. One of the biggest distractions that often stop productive people is time wasters.

Example: I once knew a man who had nothing exciting in his life to do. Whenever, I was at home working on some very important assignments that had deadlines to meet for my job, this man would stop by unannounced and say that he just wanted to say hello and to see how I was doing. I told him that I was very busy because I had some important assignments that were due on my manager's desk the very next morning, but this man would ignore me and keep on talking, and talking and talking. Well, I ended up working the entire night because this man became an obstacle to me.

I had no choice but to deal with this obstacle. So, I chose to lock my door and never to let that man in to my house whenever I was working at home. The man was an obstacle for me because he did not respect and value my time or anyone else's.

It is imperative that you take an observation of all obstacles that are holding you back, then, find a solution for removing your obstacles. If you don't face your obstacles, you will never accomplish anything.

A formula that is used for dealing with obstacles is to:

- Challenge the future by competing against the past.
- Focus on an opportunity rather than on the problem.
- Choose your own direction – rather than climb on the bandwagon; and
- Aim high, aim for something that will make a difference rather than for something that is "safe and easy to do."
- Count your blessings, not your troubles.
- Learn to live one day at a time.
- Practice the "Do it now" habit.
- Never quit or give up regardless of the obstacles or circumstances that hinder you.

A fighter trains very hard to master all of the techniques and fundamentals that are involved in the game of boxing. If the fighter does not train properly and become disciplined, the fighter will not become a champion inside of the ring.

Your opponent is the obstacle that stands in your path to stop you and keep you from winning the match. However, if you work very hard and develop the habit and action that allow you to counterattack the moves of your challenger, you have a greater chance for winning the fight.

I can remember as a little boy on my way to school, I often met bullies who wanted to pick on me or fight me for no reason. I was a very shy, timid kid who never bothered with anyone, but my parents prepared me for my obstacles in school by teaching me how to think for myself and to defend myself if someone tried to harm me.

My mother told me to always walk in well lighted places and to let my teachers how if there was trouble. One day out of nowhere, I was confronted by a bully. There was nowhere to run or to hide. I was forced to face my obstacle. We threw punches at each other. It was a nasty fight. I lost a couple of teeth, but so did the bully. When the dust settled, neither of us wanted any more. The bully moved out of my way. A line of mutual respect was created and we finally became friends.

That day, I learned something very valuable. You can run away from your problems, but that doesn't mean that your problems will run away from you.

Life isn't always easy. It's full of ups and downs. The only thing that we can do is prepare ourselves to the best of our abilities. Do you see the big picture? The big picture is the end result. The big picture gives us the attitude, motivation, and momentum to move ahead.

Opportunities await us, but anything that is worthwhile is certainly worth fighting for. Don't give up because your obstacle looks like a giant and you feel like a grasshopper. Don't give up because you're tired, weak, and your pace seems slow. Just keep your focus and fight. You will succeed, even if it takes another blow.

Success is seeing yourself as a winner regardless of the obstacles and distractions that are telling you to throw in the towel.

A fighter trains very hard to master all of the techniques and fundamentals that are involved in the game of boxing. If the fighter does not train properly and become disciplined, the fighter will not become a champion inside of the ring.

Your opponent is the obstacle that stands in your path to stop you and keep you from winning the match. However, if you worked very hard and developed the habit and action that will allow you to counterattack the moves of your challenger, you will have a greater chance of winning the fight.

Life places obstacles along our paths. In order for us to remove these obstacles, we need persistence, drive, focus and supreme confidence in our abilities to stay the course. No matter where you go, there will always be obstacles along the way. Don't give up.

Chapter 4–
"Setbacks and Disappointments"

I don't know of anyone who has not had to deal with setbacks or disappointments in life. Everyone will face challenges and disappointments in their lives at some point and time, but how you handle the unexpected and how fast you are able to bounce back will depend on your attitude. Many college graduates and MBA's can't find jobs. One of the main reasons is because of their negative attitudes and their unwillingness to take a lower level job which they might consider "beneath" them.

I think that's precisely one of the reasons which underlines why some people quickly become millionaires and others don't. The ones with the right attitudes are willing to take any job no matter how humbling it may be just for the chance to work and earn money is welcomed.

When you possess a negative attitude, you look for reasons to reject such positions – and spend months, even years trying to collect unemployment benefits. The people with positive attitudes use what they have to create their own career and that's how many millionaires are produced in our society. The men and women with wit, who possesses positive attitudes about winning, are the real opportunity makers who've learned how to capitalize on the smallest chance.

There are no bad jobs, only bad attitudes. Change your attitude, take any job,, and do it extremely well, or as best as you can. Your results will be amazing. The right attitude can create job success which translates into job security and your life will be totally different.

Sometimes the worst situations can produce the best medicine for your life. Every individual on this planet should be treated with respect and dignity because we are all important. All of us are unique in our special way. There will never be another exactly like you. Your life has a purpose and when you discover your purpose or design for this life, you will be fulfilled and the void or emptiness that you may feel will automatically be removed.

When you are passionate and excited about your life, you wake up in the mornings like a winning prize fighter ready and eager to defeat his next opponent. When you see yourself as a winner, you look for ways to eliminate obstacles and setbacks.

Does everybody have setbacks and disappointments? Yes, some may have them more often than others, but we all have them. The way that you handle them is what separates the rubber from the road. If you are a thinker, you will come up with your own list of strategies for eliminating the setbacks and disappointments that keep getting in your way.

I will never forget Uncle Roy. Uncle Roy grew up in the country near a small town called Gilmer, TX. He grew up with setbacks and disappointments because his family was poor. After leaving the military, he looked for work, but could not find any. He did some odd jobs and worked a lot of part-time jobs, but soon he became very discouraged because every time he went out to an interview for a full-time job, he was turned down. He had a family and his bills were stacked up. He finally got a full-time job only to be laid off. He said that he felt like giving up because of his job situation.

One day, he woke up with an idea. His idea was to write out a plan to move to a larger city so that he could start over again with a fresh new beginning. He and his family moved to the city. He searched endlessly for a good job, but again, he had no luck. One evening just as he arrived home after picking his kids up at school, he decided to take his suit to a new cleaner. He took his best suit to the cleaners, which was far away.

When he returned a week later to pick up his suit, he was shocked to learn that the suit was lost. Uncle Roy said to himself, "I'm going to find me a quality cleaner near by or I'll open up one myself. Out of his disappointment and frustrations, he decided to open up a dry cleaner.

Uncle Roy opened up twelve dry cleaners and became the first millionaire in our family. When you learn to face your setbacks and disappointments, you can overcome them by looking for positive ideas and solutions.

The task will not become overwhelming or impossible to endure if we tackle every obstacle with a well written thought out plan. When you start your new career or launch your business, you have confidence and an "I expect to win" attitude.

Life brings about change. Our bodies changes. The world changes. Nothing stays the same forever. Sometimes, these changes become challenges, setbacks, and disappointments, but we can rise to the occasion and turn these tough times into opportunities because the possibilities are unlimited when we cultivate the right attitude. Your attitude can motivate you to take action if you are convinced that actions will help you to become successful and you see a positive outcome.

I do not know any successful person that is known for having a bad attitude about winning. A winner enjoys winning. A winner easily adapts to winning. In fact, a winner looks beyond disappointments and setbacks because he or she is focused so strongly on winning that they expect to win every time even though they may not always win. They possess an attitude that lets everyone know that they expect to win. See yourself as a winner who expects to win regardless of setbacks and disappointments.

Chapter 5 –

"A craftsman needs the right tools"

A craftsman is basically someone who possesses a special skill or experience acquired over years of patient activity. In order for a craftsman to do his work, he must have the tools of his trade. If there are no tools, the craftsman will be delayed or held up from successfully completing his work.

When you discover your design or purpose, it is important to know what resources or tools that are available to help you become more successful. It may take some time to locate what is needed in your life, but once you find them, you will gain self-confidence and your attitude will catapult to higher level of mental toughness.

Your attitude is a transmitter that sends signals to everyone that you meet. These signals can be negative or positive based on your ability to perform and how you think or feel about yourself.

No one can conquer their fears without getting themselves ready to face them and by learning to be like a craftsman. You must put in the time to study, work and perform in order to capture the attention of those that search for leaders of their industry or trade.

The more you do, the more you know, the more you are willing to learn, the more confident you will become and the higher your attitude will soar.

Someone once said to me, your attitude will determine your attitude. One of the greatest tools that every craftsman must have in order to be successful is possess a positive attitude.

A craftsman needs the right tools. How does a con artist get good at his craft? He practices it everyday or as many times as necessary until he has it down to a pat. I think that the more you practice, the better you will become.

I've heard people talk about the jobs that will be cut and the evening news shows announcing layoffs of thousands of people. There has certainly been insecurity in the labor force. Some people panic and nearly go into shock when this comes close to them.

These things can really stress people out. Some people have even committed suicide. It's even touchy to discuss job uncertainty with family and friends. Everyone wants to go into denial or hide by avoiding such talk, but will these actions make your dilemma change or go away? In actuality, no it will not.

Whether we like or not, people are probably being laid off by the thousands in a good economy as well as a bad economy. You can expect this to happen because economic trends will continue for years to come and they will always fluctuate up and down

I learned in Economics that we should always study the market to learn everything we can about how people survive and how they make a living from day to day.

A successful craftsman is prepared to pay the price. He or she may spend hundreds of hours working with individuals, training, seminars, testing, courses, etc. so that a complete understanding and sensitivity for every instrument, tool, or machine can be used for precise and accurate specifications. Your tools include everything that's needed for your success. The mark of a successful craftsman is excellence.

A master craftsman will always have an attitude towards excellence in his or her field, especially their attitude towards the people who are the very best at what they are doing or planning to do.

I've met many successful people and one of the things that I've noticed is that they all have a great admiration and respect for the top performers in their field or industries. When you have a desire to be the best, you will move into the direction of what you admire the most. As you grow and hang around people that you look up to and admire for being the best in their field, you will suddenly become like them.

Just as a craftsman uses his tools for perfection, you must use your tools so that you can become the best at whatever you choose to become. Let your attitude toward excellence take you beyond your limits so that you can reach for the stars and make your dreams a reality.

Select the top people in your field for role models. As you begin to grow, compare your accomplishments to the accomplishments of the top people that you've selected.

A lot of people who work at their jobs do not care about being the best and being at the top in their industry. They are satisfied with being at the bottom of the barrel, but don't let that affect you.

People may give up, but don't you give up. Never become jealous or envious of the ability or success of others. Instead, take notes, emulate their best qualities, then, give it your best.

Remember, as a craftsman becomes a master, you can become a winner and discover your design or purpose in life.

Chapter 6 –

"My grandfather
was a farmer"

As a young boy at the age of 9, I can remember hanging around my grandfather and watching him work very hard in the fields harvesting crops for our family. I enjoyed living in the country and eating the fresh produce that came from grand pa Charlie's farm.

Every year, he would fertilize the soil, then, plant the seeds into the ground. He had rows of corn, peas, squash, tomatoes, cucumbers, potatoes, onions, beets, cabbage, collard greens, turnip greens, cantaloupes, and watermelons, and etc.

If you want to improve your knowledge base, you must examine yourself and start thinking about your mental capacity. An unintelligent person is someone that's lacking in knowledge or uninformed about many things. Some people become embarrassed or simply shut down when they feel that they are surrounded by people that they consider smart or highly educated.

One way to overcome these negative feelings is to read more often. As my grandfather planted seeds to harvest large crops, we should invest seeds of concern and love for others, study time, knowledge and education, family time, quiet time, volunteering and giving to the needy, research, environmental advances, elderly care, teen suicides, battered and abused victims, and etc.

You are not truly successful if you cannot find a way to give back to others by planting seeds into the hearts and souls of men. There will always be hurting people around, therefore, there will always be plenty of fields to plant seeds in and allow your crops time to harvest. The more seeds that you sow, the more plants you will grow.

My grandfather taught me how beautiful the earth can be when you take the time to prepare the ground, plant your seeds and allow the growth process to take place and reproduce from its own element.

Today is not that much different from the time that my grandfather was farming years ago. Everyone wants to win big in life. We all want to achieve a high level of success. We will want everything that we put hard work and sweat into to work.

My grandfather, "Grandpa Charlie," had a natural talent for training animals, making home remedies from organic plants and harvesting large crops in the fields, and landscaping. People from all over would come by the farm to see his work. His vegetable garden and fruit trees were beautiful. His lawn and landscaping work was amazingly attractive. The animals on the farm were obedient and very well trained. The local stores were receptive to receiving fresh produce from him.

I can even remember people coming out to visit Grandpa Charlie to ask questions and take notes on: How to harvest a successful crop? How to grow the biggest and sweetest watermelons? How to treat your soil?

One gentleman asked Grandpa Charlie what did he do to make his watermelons so good and sweet? Grandpa Charlie looked at the man and said, "I soak my melon seeds in sugar every year before planting them in the ground. When my melons grow they are always big and sweet."

Grandpa Charlie was a successful farmer. We grew up with the best of everything that his farm could produce.

Now was Grandpa Charlie lucky? No, I believe that Grandpa Charlie was blessed with good health, knowledge, and a good work ethic. When you're successful, people say that you're lucky. To me luck is what happens when preparation meet opportunity.

Did you know that countless numbers of people are sitting around waiting for a lucky break? I don't believe that people have lucky breaks. I believe that success comes when we work hard like Grandpa Charlie and prepare ourselves for the day that our plane will arrive. When it lands, be ready to board that plane so that you can pursue your "destiny."

If you can come up with a good idea, money will automatically come. All you need is a new piece of knowledge, a new idea, a new insight, and the willingness and the ability to apply it in the marketplace, and soon you will be an overnight success.

A farmer learns how to plant seeds in the right season for a successful harvest. You must invest knowledge, study, training and hard work into yourself in order to harvest your talent and potential abilities.

Chapter 7 –

"Your image is important"

When you look at yourself in the mirror, what do you see? Do you see someone that you like or do you see someone that you hate? Most of us have encountered a trauma, rejection, disaster, pain, bitterness or disappointment of some sort. The truth is that some of us were able to get past it and some of us were not.

I believe that if you can somehow find a way to look beyond your past and look towards your future, you can bury the past and walk in positive expectancy about your future.

Sometimes, it is difficult to move beyond your past because friends, relatives, or old acquaintances may try to bring up negatives so that they can tear down your self-esteem. The only way that some people know how to keep you down is to put your past in the streets. Here are a few ideas that may help you overcome this problem so that you can move ahead to the future.

One way is to put together some affirmations that will promote positive self-talk. For example, a biblical affirmation might be, "I can do all things through Christ who strengthens me."

Another affirmation might be, "I am a winner and people enjoy my company."

Create your own affirmations and read them to yourself every morning before leaving home for work or you can read them every night before bedtime.

Another thing that you can do is change your appearance. If you want to work at a bank, you can dress professional and act as though you are a successful banking executive.

You might consider this an extreme measure, but it has worked for me. Try dressing up in an attire for your particular profession or trade. Example, if you want to become a doctor, put on a doctor's uniform with a stethoscope around your neck. Have someone take a picture of you and blow the picture up into a large poster, then put the picture up in your bedroom or hallway so that you can look at the picture daily or as often as possible.

The picture helps motivate you to change your self-image so that you can start pursuing your goals. There are numerous ways to change your self-image.

You can even record your voice and listen to it daily on the way to work. You can read some positive affirmations out loud and record them on your CD or DVD. Just do something positive that will inspire you and lift up your self-esteem

The last idea is to hang out with successful people. Attend conferences and go to lunch with them.

Your company or environment can have an affect on your life. Take note and look for things that can help you to change your self-image.

Also, check out the people that you hang around with and observe appearances, negative images and attitudes that may be affecting you.

If you want people to take you serious, you must have a good perception of yourself. How people receive you will reflect how people deal with you. You can train people to think the way that you want them to when you make them think about who you think you are.

You need to know that you know that you have what it takes to be successful. Then, you will automatically develop a healthy self-image. When you possess a healthy self-image and believe in yourself, people will believe in you.

Chapter 8 –

"Do you have a Dream or a Vision?"

You've got to have a dream. If you don't have a dream, you may not have a future. Success is obtaining the unobtainable or doing something that no one else believed you had the guts to do. Competition involves being the best you can be and refusing to worry about what others think.

Use what talents you possess. If you use what you've got, you may discover a well of unlimited potential. Dare to dream and capture the universe of supply and demand. Unlimited Potential is usually stored up in an individual who never used it.

Where does the world's greatest talent reside? It lies in the graveyards. Where's the world's greatest talent at? It is in the graveyards, because too many people leave this world never knowing or using their full potential. Isn't it a shame?

If the sun is shining in your life, your future will be very bright. Your path will be clear. But, if the sun goes down in your life, it means that you have no dream or ambition to become a champion. One good idea can turn on the light of hope and positive expectancy in your world.

If you have a dream or vision, you will be inspired to keep moving ahead in your quest to venture out and make things happen.

Think Big! Dream Big! It is your choice. It is your idea. No one can steal your dream. Just dream and visualize what you want in life. When you can see it, feel it, and believe in it, the manifestation of your dream will begin to take root and your dreams will become a reality. If you dare to dream, your vision will become your future.

I try to inspire everyone that I meet to dream big because I believe that dreams will transform your mind to allow it to produce ideas, strategies, information, creativity, and solutions for solving problems in your life and others.

More job lay-offs are coming. You must take action today. Dare to dream! You must make a quality decision about your future. Don't procrastinate if you realize your potential abilities and the opportunities that are facing you.

What's holding you back? Sometimes, fear of the unknown is the biggest factor that causes a lot of people to stay in a rut and to give up so easily. In order to capture your future, make sure you got all of the facts, study your market, analyze it, then reach beyond the clouds, and pull down a handful of stars. In order to achieve the obtainable, you must set your goals high enough to reach the unobtainable. I believe if you can dream about it, you will see it, then, you will achieve it. Nearly all great leaders have dreams and visions.

A dream can motivate you to a level of high expectation. Doubt, negativism, unbelief, and uncertainty will short-circuit your ability to dream and put out your flames of a burning desire that's needed to launch you forward regardless of criticism, circumstances or hindrances in life.

Dreaming big dreams allow you to release your God-given potential. Your potential is unlimited. Dare to dream so that you may release it. If you dare to dream, you may be surprised to discover what your design or purpose for this life is waiting within you to be revealed.

Chapter 9 –

"You need a goal"

The Importance of Setting Goals

I've had to deal with obstacles and challenges since elementary school. In fact, I can remember being picked on by bullies at school and coming home in the evening with my upper and lower lips being busted. Also, I can recall one fight that gave me a busted lip and when I got off the school bus to cross the highway, my grandmother and my mom greeted me and were shocked to see the blood all over my shirt and my fists were clinched as I held on to the broken teeth that were still in my hands.

Grandmother said, "Dwight, I worry about you, why do you get into fights every day at school?" I said, "I try to avoid fights, but it seems like every day someone comes after me." My grandmother prayed for me and said, "Life has many obstacles. They can cause you to give up easily or you can learn to face those obstacles and keep fighting them until you become a winner. Even if you lose the fight, you are still a winner because those bullies will respect you for not letting them run over you."

By setting goals, you can eliminate obstacles that are in your path - and turn your dreams into a reality. Your own vision of the future consists of a set of goals that is unique to you. Identifying your vision and the goals that comprise it – can provide invaluable context for your career decisions.

What motivates you?

Motivation is fuel that will carry you up the ladder of success. Your goals are what motivate you to work, to aspire, and to accomplish your dreams and visions. They help you determine the most effective career strategies and provide touchstones for your day-to-day life choices. The progress you make toward your goals will be the ultimate benchmark for assessing the performance of your skills, talents, and the development of your full potential.

The more motivated you become, the higher your determination rises, which in turn will help you to build the life you want for yourself and the people you love. If you are motivated, your personal goals and accomplishments will serve as both a roadmap and a beacon: guiding your decisions, while urging you onward as you create the future you envision.

Every delicious pie or cake is made by a recipe that includes certain ingredients that are mixed together or blended together, then placed in the oven at a certain temperature and cooked. The outcome is amazing because the flavor and aroma fills an entire room. The sweet smell of success in your life, works in a similar fashion because it captures the hearts and attitudes of people that are around you.

"The main ingredient or fuel for success is Motivation." Any man or woman that has no motivation in their life is like an automobile without fuel and no driver. In order to become more successful in your life, you must be motivated. A question that is often asked is what is motivation and how can I become motivated?

Motivation is learning to dream and applying thoughts and actions to your dreams along with determination and belief that moves you forward despite the obstacles and setbacks that often get into our way.

One of the best ways to develop your motivation is to first think about what you would really like to become or accomplish in life.

The next step is to create a mental image or picture for your mind to view on a daily basis. After you've done this, meditate on your vision or dream and see yourself as you would like to become.

Examine yourself and search for things that motivate and inspire you to take action. Example: I enjoy seafood dining, therefore, I may place a picture of my favorite seafood restaurant on my desk or wall.

Every time I accomplish an important task. I will reward myself by taking my family and me to a really nice seafood restaurant. You might enjoy golfing, hunting, or etc. so look for something that gets you excited.

Chapter 10 –

"You need a plan and a strategy"

A man with no plan is like someone lost and stranded on a desert island. If you want to escape, you must have a plan and a strategy or suffer disaster.

It is not impossible to achieve excellence in everything you do. Learn from your mistakes so that you can make your life an outstanding work of art.

Think Big! Dream Big! Before you can think big or dream big, you must have a plan and a strategy. Once you create a good plan and a strategy, your dreams can become a reality.

The first step is to think about your goal, then write it down on paper. Make sure that goal is realistic, attainable and visually clear in your mind. After you write your goal down, write your reasons and the benefits from achieving this goal.

Step two. List your fears and setbacks. What's hindering you from conquering this goal?

Step three. Write out a plan and strategy for going to the top. What can you do to become successful in your career or finances? Try to think of things that will help you achieve the level of success that you desire. As you write and list your strategies, you will begin to solve problems that were impossibilities.

Step four. After you write out your plan and list all of your strategies, you should then carefully have something to do each day that will guide you on a path of consistency. You can call this list, "your things to do today list." At the end of the day, draw a line through or underline each accomplishment for the day.

As you begin to accomplish your goals, you will become motivated and focused. Remember, all you have to do is to get started. The sooner you put together a plan and a strategy, the more successful you will become.

There are countless numbers of people that do not have a plan. Why are there so many people that do not have a plan? Can you think of a reason why these people do not have a plan? I cannot give you the exact truth, but I can say that there is no excuse for not having a plan.

A good plan is your blueprint for laying a solid foundation in your life. Before a builder can build a house, he must first build a solid foundation or the house will not have the strength to last.

A storm or heavy wind may cause it to collapse or be destroyed. Please, do not take this information for granted. It will only take a few short minutes out of your time. Why put things off for tomorrow when you can conquer them today?

The purpose for executing a plan is to actually develop a step-by-step strategy for overcoming obstacles and achieving a particular goal.

When you have a careful, written plan, you will discover that most problems and obstacles may never surface or materialize because your focus on the plan will give you the ability to concentrate on details and activities that are defined in your plan.

It will also require discipline and toughness on your part in areas that demand mental focus in order to succeed. Have you ever been lost and traveling around in circles? It's easy to get lost when you're not using a plan as your guidepost.

The best strategy is to work hard on your plan and include every alternative so that you won't end up on a dead-end street. Your plan should steer you into the path of leadership, commitment and a motivation to take action.

Chapter 11 –

"The rewards of simplicity"

What do you do for a living? Can you list at least ten benefits or rewards that you've received from doing what you do for a living? If you've listed ten, which one is the most rewarding? Life is too short not to be having fun. Believe it or not, our best work takes place when we enjoy it.

Most of us have to work for a living. For some people, it is extremely difficult to hold down a job or to successfully advance.

Another question to ask yourself, is … "Do you have a less than perfect job or income base?

There are many things that one can factor into your equation and making it very complex. Have you considered the thought that you may actually hate your job so much that its affected your attitude and the people that are around you.

You must do your best to keep things simple. Don't let your life become complicated. You can't put out a fire by adding more fuel to the flames.

Simplicity offers greatest rewards. What comes to your mind when you see or hear the word simplicity? Simplicity is realizing that life can be fun if you find a way to keep it simple and painless. Let's think about your job or career for a moment. What do you enjoy doing so much that you would be willing to do for free? What makes you dream, think and smile whenever you see someone doing it?

What do you love doing and constantly think about it all the time? Every time you think about it, or see someone else doing it, do you go, "that's me?"

Success starts first with making the most of what you already have.

I remember a time when I hated my job as a janitor. But one morning after I arrived to church, I heard a minister preach a message entitled, "Take this job ... And Love it." I really didn't want to hear that particular message because I was thinking about quitting. I hated the job because the work was overwhelming and the hours were very long.

As I listened carefully to the message, I saw myself as the man he was talking about. The minister looked directly at me and said, "Whatever you think about and focus on the most, you will attract that very thing into your life.

The entire message got my attention. I quickly made a decision to change my attitude and to think about the things that I really wanted. Everything in my life started to change. It was amazing for me to see and experience success in areas of my life that I never dreamed would be possible.

My attitude changed and as a direct result of that change, I achieved more goals. Simplicity is the reward of a man or woman who discovers their passion, design, or purpose in life. A fish on land look odd, but once the fish is placed back into the ocean, its brilliance kicks in and the simplicity of his design allows him to swim in the water like no other creature.

When you know what your design and purpose is in life, you will perform at a higher level of potential. Because you're in your element just as the fish was, now you can be what you were created to be. Everything will become simple when you release the potential within you to be activated and by learning to be you, not someone else.

Chapter 12 –
"Success breeds success"

Continued success is the results of continued work in progress. If the grass is greener on the other side, make sure you're prepared to pay for a higher water bill when you get there.

When you're successful, you will have something in common with other successful people. Its hard work, but the rewards and fruits of your labor far outweigh the benefits.

I once read a scripture in the Bible that stated, "The lazy man long for many things, but his hands refuse to work. He is greedy to get, while the godly love to give!
Proverbs 21:25, 26

No pain, no gain. Work is not hard when you are enjoying it. When people enjoy their work, you can sometimes sense it through their attitudes that are projected.

I would rather work with people who like what they do than to work around people who hate what they do.

How do you feel about yourself on the inside? The way that you feel about yourself projects an attitude within you that will attract or repel others.

Over the years, I've met people that were unattractive as far as physical appearance is concerned, but the attitude of these amazing people captured my attention.

I believe that the inner beauty that's on the inside of them pulled in attractive successful people. These people seemed to have other people following them around and wanting to be their friends. I believe that these people had an aura about them that projects self-confidence and success.

Success breeds success! You've probably heard this before, but it's true. Everyone or almost everyone enjoys being around people that are successful.

Winners think about winning all the time. Winners enjoy winning. Winning offers a feeling of satisfaction and fulfillment to those that thirst for it. You can't find a winner that wants to be on a losing team. If you are a winner and you enjoy winning, you look for opportunities that prepare you for winning.

Successful people enjoy helping others because they know that it's important to teach people how to set goals. Every time you achieve worthy goals, you will receive recognition from someone.

People want attention. They want to be noticed. They want to receive honor and credit for personal achievements.

God's greatest gift to you is your hidden potential. Your gift to God is to use what you got and use it to the best of your ability.

Chapter 13 –

"The heart of a winner"

M any people create a living but do not create a lifestyle for following generations. You must create a legacy behind you. Your kids and grandkids should not have to worry about jobs.

You must be able to distinguish between a need and a want. Pay cash or do without.

The cycle of failure

- Keeping up with the Joneses.
- No liquidity.
- No financial assets.
- Great consumer debt.
- No time for self or family.
- Low self-esteem.

Success is an attitude. Successful people have positive attitudes. Negative people think that they have all the answers to why nothing good can ever happen.

Are you afraid of change? You should be afraid of staying in the same rut and doing the same thing over and over again, but expecting new results.

Building the foundation for success. There is a strategy for creating your circle of wealth. You must have a complete game plan that includes the 5 ingredients of success.

- First, change your attitude.
- Get specialized knowledge.
- Use the tools of a pro.
- Invest your money wisely.
- Wise counselors can power your master mind group.
- You need a good plan or strategy if you want to win.

Your success will depend on your attitude. The smarter you are the more money you will make. When your attitude is bad, you see no future. But, when you possess a positive attitude, you will dream.

Just ask yourself two questions? What is my dream? What do I want my life to look like in 5 years from now? Someone once told me dreams without action stays dreams.

Success is an attitude that follows you to your destination and produces a victory in your life. The greatest battle that you will ever have is your mind. Your mind carries negative thoughts and positive thoughts. When the positives win over the negatives, the results or outcome will be a winning attitude.

A winning attitude gives us ideas and solutions for achieving our goals. A winning attitude also gives us the confidence that we need in order to conquer our fears and the determination to persist until we succeed.

How can you expect to win in life if you don't possess a winning attitude? Coaches work with athletes on a consistent basis to develop the attitude and work habits for becoming champions both on and off the field.

I can now really appreciate all of the coaches that I grew up with – because they taught me respect, hard work, discipline, determination, and to have an attitude that says I'm a winner.

I will never forget Coach Sizemore, Coach Byrd, Coach Locke, Coach Hough, Coach Bill, and Coach Charles Holmes, Sr. These men were leaders who taught us how to win in sports, but also how to win in life.

Chapter 14 –

"Are you a leader or a follower"

Are you a leader or a follower?

Let's start first of all by thinking about the word Leader. What do you think of when you hear the word Leader? Who do you think of when you hear the word Leader?

A leader is a person who leads, guides, directs or someone who has authority or influence to a large degree.

Over the years, I've studied many leaders and the attitudes and habits that they possess. There are certain traits that I've observed and found out that the one thing that they have in common is most of them are focused more on their talents and gifts instead of the negative attitudes and influences of negative people. They were determined to meet their deadlines and accomplish their goals.

Now, let's think about the word Follower for a moment. What comes to your mind when you hear the word Follower? Do you consider yourself to be a follower? What does the word follower actually mean?

A follower is considered as a person who follows the opinions or teachings of others. A follower can also be a person who imitates another.

There is a process that one must undergo before he or she can become a great leader. The first step is to become a good follower. You cannot become a great leader until you first become a good follower.

The words leader and follower both intertwine or connect with one another. They connect with each other, and they also complement each other.

If you want to be a leader, you've got to build you. When you invest in yourself, you're being a leader. An example might be education.

It cost lots of money, time, and sacrifice, but it pays off by helping you become a leader. In fact, the best investment that you could make is an investment in you. When you invest in you, you are also investing in your self-worth. As a leader, you must become a student of leadership.

It takes a good follower to develop into a good leader. In other words, you must be coachable, positive, optimistic, enthusiastic, a good communicator, a good teacher, duplicator, strong work ethic, and the ability to stay focused.

Developing your leadership qualities and skills will help you increase your tenacity. A good leader will not easily give up on anything because he or she is determined to achieve the goals or dreams in life.

When people are inspired by you, they do their work or task to the best of their ability, one can say that this is the accomplishment of a leader.

A leader possesses the ability to influence others. If at all possible, take the classes, get the training and exposure that will help you develop the leader that is within.

Challenge yourself to grow and discover the most effective way to understand the power of influence and think of things that were inspired by a person or an event. Think about the teacher, preacher, doctor, manager, co-worker, friend or neighbor who influenced you in a powerful way.

My college business professor, Dr. Lorene B. Holmes, would always tell each of her students to be the best. She inspired me so much that I would daydream in class and visualize myself achieving my goals and becoming very successful. Dr. Holmes was the kind of leader that that pushed me and others to use our full potential.

Another example of a great leader in my family was my grandmother, Ms. Ludie Wright. We called her, Mama Ludie. Grandmother was not able to complete high school, but she was a very smart, intelligent woman who could talk to anyone on any subject. Her insight and wisdom was so amazing that her children, grandchildren, and great grandchildren would come from around the country just to sit down and ask her for advice so that they could get a solution for their problems.

As a child, I did not like working in the field harvesting crops, but my grandmother inspired me to become a hard worker and go on to college and graduate as a top academic student. Even though she is no longer with us, I often reflect back to her talks and lessons from the Book of Proverbs and all of a sudden, I'm ready to tackle another obstacle. She was a leader in my family and today we are very thankful for her strong influence.

Chapter 15 –

"Success is the best revenge"

Are you driven to succeed? Do you feel that your family and friends have turned their backs on you and deserted you? Do you feel isolation and rejection? If you have answered yes to all of these questions, you're probably right. It's time to stop complaining and feeling sorry for yourself.

There are always advantages to look for in every situation. There is a scripture in the book of Proverbs that states, "A poor man is hated by everyone, including his own family."

When you are hated, no one wants to be close to you or around you. This can actually be an advantage because you can work quietly. There are no distractions because no one wants to be around you, it is beneficial for you to get more things done. You can work as long as you want to.

You can use your time wisely and accomplish more when people aren't hanging around and getting in your way. You should find some positive things to do so that you will not sit around and worry about who came to see you and who did not.

If you worry about people all of the time, it means that you simply do not have a life. You should utilize your time to accomplish more goals.

Some people commit suicide because they feel that their life is not important and that they do not have a purpose in life. My college professor, Dr. Lorene B. Holmes, would always say to our class, "Work hard and be the best!" It takes hard work and dedication to be the best at what you do.

If you waste your time sitting around complaining, you will miss out on valuable opportunities,. Everyone likes a winner. When you're more successful, people aspire to be like you. They want to meet you and be around you. Some people will even move to a new city so that they can be near the winners of a championship.

Instead of hating people and thinking of ways to get back at them, it is better to work on improving your skills which represent the training and experiences that you've gathered over the years so that you can pursue your dreams and achieve your goals.

When you acquire success, you will attract honor, respect, fame, and fortune. Your world can become interesting, exciting, and fun. You can go places you've never dreamed of, you can live the best, wear the best, drive the best, and experience the best that life has to offer.

Chapter 16 –

"Invest in yourself"

An investor must learn to cultivate the right attitude if he or she plans to be successful in the stock market. It takes research, study, and timing because a volatile market can shift at any time. An investor must be prepared to go with the momentum of the market.

You are an investor, even though you may not buy, sell, and trade stocks. The success of your financial future will be measured on how well you invest your money, time, and resources.

The best investment that you could ever make is in yourself and your personal well-being. When you develop a positive mental attitude, and a healthy self-esteem, you will see yourself and your efforts as worthwhile. You will automatically look for ways to deepen or improve your knowledge base.

Everyone that I know and people all over the world, are searching for a great investment. People are looking for an investment that will yield a high rate of return. Their questions might be focused on, how many shares are needed to be purchased in order to receive a dividend?

Again, I must remind you that you are the best investment. There are no limits placed on your net worth potential except for the self-imposed boundaries that may be harvested by a negative attitude and a low self-esteem. No one on earth knows about the limitless capacity of potential that is within you. Do you know that you are the hottest investment on the face of this planet?

A question that may pop up in your mind is, "If I'm so hot, why isn't I benefitting and receiving the monetary reward?" To answer your question, I think it's because you've looked and searched everywhere except from within yourself.

You are unique because God created you with a design and purpose to fulfill in this life. You were born with talents, skills, and untapped potential. That means that you have unlimited potential.

It takes boldness, hard work, good timing, and business savvy to become a good investor. If you invest in yourself, and get into position, you can then tap into endless opportunities that will allow you to grow both personally and professionally.

I would like to recommend the following ideas and resources for helping you tap into your potential.

1. Online educational training and self-development courses.
2. Local programs (Community Colleges, Universities and Training Seminars).
3. Private research in Public Libraries.
4. Biblical economic courses.
5. Books, CD's, DVD's.
6. Job-training opportunities.
7. Correspondence courses.
8. Join a local Toastmasters organization. Regardless of what field you choose.
   When you learn to speak clearly and confidently, it will help you.
9. Take a class that will further your career.
10. Get in the best shape of your life.
11. Get organized.
12. Eliminate stress, lighten up, and invest in others.
13. Be more thankful.

14. **Find** a mentor, advisor, coach, or partner to improve your game.
15. **Make** someone's day everyday.
16. **Find** out what motivates you.
17. **Learn** how to motivate others.
18. **Be a** mentor for someone else.
19. **Send** out more thank you notes.
20. **Break** a bad habit or start a good one.
21. **Walk** more, talk more, and read more,
22. **Read** a book a month.
23. **Read** your Bible everyday.
24. **Get** rid of all obstacles that are holding you back your success.
25. **Become** a better listener.
26. **Smile** more and stay humble.
27. **Reward** yourself when you achieve your goals.
28. **Volunteer** in your church or community.
29. **Eat** healthy, exercise more, and drink more water.
30. **Set** daily, weekly, monthly, and yearly goals.
31. **Create** a strategy and a plan for achieving success.
32. **Work** hard at having a gratitude attitude. Don't let bitterness and resentment rob you of your valuable time.
33. **Avoid** jealousy and negative thinking.
34. **Maintaining** a positive attitude, don't talk failure.
35. **Don't** procrastinate, develop a do it now habit.
36. **Remember**, you are an investor, so keep learning, growing and investing in yourself.

The benefits that you'll gain from investing into yourself will increase your knowledge base, boost your attitude and the rewards will be phenomenal.

When you invest in yourself, you can live your dream, achieve your goals, and define your purpose. The results of investing into yourself can position you to live the best, wear the best, drive the best, and experience the best that life has to offer.

If you are not willing to invest in yourself so that you can risk the unusual, you will have to settle for the ordinary.

Chapter 17 –

"Success is an Attitude"

Your attitude is your most important asset. You will not attract people if your attitude is bad. A bad attitude will repel people instead of drawing people. People will support you when they believe in you.

Your attitude is the result of learning of learning from mistakes, failures and setbacks, then programming your mind to react intelligently so that you can begin a process of growth and development that is needed in order to succeed.

There is a scripture in the Bible that reads: "This book of the law shall not depart out of thy mouth, but thou shall meditate therein, day and night that thou mayest observe to do according to all that is written therein, for then thou shalt make thy way prosperous and thou shall have good success. Joshua 1:8

When you program your mind with quality information and allow your mind to process it, you will automatically develop an attitude that will cause you to release creative ideas for problem solving and lead you into a path of success.

"Success is an Attitude," use it to discover your passion.

What's an attitude? An attitude is your mental position or feeling regarding something that is factual in your life.

How do you feel about yourself on the inside? Some of the most unattractive people in the world are the ones that appeal to the majority of the people.

There is an aura that they project and it attracts people. That aura is simply an attitude that comes to mind when you think about people that stand out from the crowd. Some people prefer to use the word charisma. Many successful leaders have been listed as men and women with charisma.

There are many great people in our society that have captured our hearts by their charisma and their passion to fulfill their purpose in life.

You can call it whatever you want, but I believe that our attitudes break us or make us. There are certain people that leave a lasting impression on us. You might say that it's their charisma. I say it's their attitude.

The leaders that I mentioned earlier possess the same characteristics that allowed people to sense an attitude of self-confidence, a strong vision that proposed a future better than the status quo, the ability to articulate the vision, strong convictions in the vision, and the willingness to enact radical change. When you have a positive attitude and a strong conviction, you can use your passion to generate enthusiasm, let your body language speak instead of words and draw people in by creating a bond that inspires others to follow and this will in turn bring out the potential by tapping into their emotions.

There are even some unattractive people that appeal to many because there is an aura that they project that attracts people. This aura is simply an attitude that comes from within and projects outwardly. You have it. Everyone has it, but it's up to you to reach inside of yourself and project it.

Chapter 18 –
"Positive reflections"

My mother, Mrs. Jerlene Jeffery, had the challenge of raising four children. She was a single parent with no transportation. There was a time when we were children and we ran out of food. We lived outside of town, far in the country. My mother left us with my grandmother so that she could go into town and buy us some groceries.

She walked 5 miles to get us some groceries, but sometimes people would stop and give her a ride on the way home, but this particular day, no one stopped to give her a ride, so she walked 5 miles all the way back home with a sack full of groceries in one hand and a gallon of milk in the other. Mother faced many challenges and obstacles, but she made sure that we were never hungry or went lacking for anything. She made sure that we had the best of everything. Mother would always tell us, "Don't worry, where there is a will, there is a way." She possessed the attitude of a winner.

Mrs. Maggie Curry "Aunt Maggie," was a courageous and persistent woman. Aunt Maggie fought her way out of an abusive marriage with her first husband. She worked very hard to get back on her feet. She learned how to drive a car at age 38 and purchased her first automobile, then, she would take us to school, church, and other activities.

Aunt Maggie worked very hard on her job to become successful and she helped take care of everyone in our family. She married an awesome man, Robert L. Curry, "Uncle Buster" and raised two sons, named Eddie and Earl. Aunt Maggie never missed a day of canning food and cooking for our entire family on each and every holiday. I salute Aunt Maggie for being a wonderful aunt and for helping me acquire a college education.

My sister, Diane and my brother, Royce, Jr., were great dancers when we were youngsters. I was not a very good dancer, but my drama teacher asked me to audition for a part in a school play. The part needed someone to be a toy robot soldier. Diane said, "Dwight, I can help. You are a stiff person, and I can easily teach you how to do a dance called the robot." Well, my drama teacher was impressed and I got the part in the play. The play was a big success, thanks to my sister, Diane. Diane had to face many hardships and issues in life, but her goal was to become a counselor and she achieved her goal. Diane was never a quitter.

Sharon, my youngest sister is the smartest of all of my siblings. Sharon had challenges in school and obstacles along the way but she would always put together a plan and a strategy for whatever she wanted to achieve or accomplish in life. Sharon became a leader on her job. She moved my mother into her home so that she could take care of her. Sharon is an inspiration to me and the rest of our family.

My first year in college was a disaster for me because my attitude was bad and so were my grades. I was placed in a class called Human Relations in Business. My professor, Dr. Lorene B. Holmes, was the kind of person that would not take no for an answer. I received a letter from the college stating that I had been placed on academic probation because of my failing grades. I said to Dr. Holmes, "You know, I don't know if I'm going to stay in school, because, things aren't working out for me, you know?!"

Dr. Holmes looked at me and said, stop saying "you know before and after every sentence." "Do you want success in your life? Dwight, if you change your attitude, you can take the lemon that's making your life sour and turn in into lemonade.

Dr. Holmes was also the first motivation speaker who got my attention in a classroom. She taught us about self-improvement, how to motivate ourselves, and how to develop a positive attitude. She also insisted that I get involved with a new program on campus called the B.E.E.P. program.

Through this program, Dr. Holmes introduced me to millionaires and business executives from around the world. Charles Brumell, V.P. for Continental Illinois National Bank of Chicago, and Joanne Robinson, Manager for the Bendix Corporation. By this time, my attitude had changed. My grades went from D's & F's to A's.

I was awarded a scholarship for having the highest grade point average in the Economics Division. I also interviewed for an engineering position with a large organization and received a job.

Thanks to Dr. Lorene B. Holmes and the executives that mentored me, my attitude changed from being negative to becoming a positive influence to others. I can honestly say that I am also an example of an attitude adjustment.

As a teacher, you are trained to notice the characteristics of a good student. Almost every student that I know who experienced success in their careers demonstrated certain characteristics in the classroom. The one thing that each of these students had in common was the fact that they were honest, respected others, maintained a good appearance, completed their work on time, spoke clearly, they were good listeners, they shared ideas, they followed directions, they were friendly, they enjoyed helping others, they were punctual, they had good behavior, they had good attendance, they used their time wisely, and each of them had a positive attitude. Here are some examples of students that exhibited a positive attitude in my classroom.

Here is an example of how someone's life changed when their attitude changed.

As a teacher, it is very difficult to motivate a student to learn if the student has a terrible attitude. I can remember when I first began teaching in Dallas, TX.

A young man was placed in my class. I was told that this young man had been kicked out of numerous schools and classes because of fighting and a negative attitude. This young man was a bully, a class clown, a trouble maker, with very poor academic skills. He was failing almost every class. I could not get him to sit still and pay attention to me. He enjoyed disrupting the class and was given a referral almost every day.

No one else wanted this young man in their classroom because he was a problem child. I felt like giving up and kicking him out of my classroom. But I was determined to hold on and give him my best. Therefore, I decided to work at changing his attitude from bad to good. This was my greatest challenge.

The first thing I did was to sit down with Jesse and ask questions about his family, his life, and why he hated school. Also, I asked him why was he angry all of the time and why he bullied his classmates. None of his classmates like him or wanted to be friends with him.

After spending time with and asking a lot of questions, I discovered that Jesse was the youngest of eight siblings and that he was often picked on at home by his older siblings. He said that he was always pushed aside and told what to do. He said, "The stronger I get, the more people I will pay back."

Jesse never studied or worked on assignments in class. He would threaten students to let him cheat off of their paper or he would beat them up after class.

I separated Jesse from the other students and began working with him and giving him extra work. If he did not do anything, he would have to stay after class and complete it. He thought that I was extremely hard on him, but I was committed to helping him achieve academic success.

It wasn't long before he started doing his work and improving on a daily basis. I would thank him each and every time that he turned in his lesson for the day. In addition to that, I also told Jesse that he was improving and that he was a smart student. He improved so much that it was hard for him to believe that he was getting better and better.

I went over his work with him and explained to him that he did not have to cheat on his test, because he was equally as smart and intelligent as the other students. When Jesse started to believe in himself, his attitude changed from bad to good. I gave an exam to the class. Jesse received a high score which was a 98.

He's never scored high in any of his classes, especially math. Some of the students were upset and told the principal that he cheated. The principal had us to give another exam and Jesse again achieved the highest math score in his class.

Jesse's mother came to school one day and told the office staff that she needed to see me. They bought her to my class room. She said, "Are you Mr. Jeffery?" I said, "Yes, I am." She shook my hand. Tears were flowing down her cheeks. She said, "I am Jesse's mother. I wanted to personally meet you and thank you, because my son, Jesse is a different person. He talks about you every night. He said you believed in him when everyone else gave up. He now helps me work around the house and he tells me that he's going to take care of me when he gets out of school because I love you mom. I was afraid that he would end up dead or in prison because of him being a trouble maker. Mr. Jeffery, Jesse now has a positive attitude about life. I appreciate you helping my son. I have three big trucks parked outside with tail gate lunches for you and your co-workers."

Jesse and his mother moved to another city. This young man became an achiever because of his attitude.

One day my wife and I decided to go out for lunch at a nearby restaurant. As we walked in, a young lady said, "Are you Mr. Jeffery?" I said, "Yes." The young lady said, the manager told me to tell you that your dinner is on the house. I found out that a former student named Joshua was responsible for everything. Joshua came up front and told us that he was motivated by me and that his life also changed because of his new attitude. "Mr. Jeffery, because of you, I now have a positive attitude and I am very excited about my future. Thank you for talking to me about my attitude and my potential. I will always be grateful to you."

Another student named Saxon always asked questions about leadership and motivation as an eighth grader. I answered as many questions as I could and shared with him the tools that are needed for motivation and for obtaining high level achievement. Saxon became an officer in the U.S.

Marine Corp. He is now married, has a good job and lives in California. His attitude has made him a success in every endeavor.

John, a former student that I had the pleasure of meeting when he was in high school, told me that he was depressed, was not interested in school, but John told me that my talk to the class about being goal-directed and motivated helped him to shift mental gears and focus on what he wanted to do by launching his career.

John graduated from high school and is attending college. He also has a job in construction management for Trinidad Medical Consultants. John is very excited about the doors of opportunity that are opening up for him. He is highly motivated and was inspiring to me the last time we ran into each other at the local store.

Andrew was a young man who worked very hard and was a 7th grade student who showed leadership and commitment. He can honestly say that he was never late for class and his assignments were always turned in on time. He would not accept anything less than an A plus.

Finally, one day, he came to my desk and told me that he knew what his purpose was and that he wanted to be a medical doctor so that he could help save lives and make a difference. It's been years since I've seen Andrew, but one day I received a letter from him, saying, that he had completed medical school and today "Dr. Andrew" is currently completing his residency at a medical facility in Dallas, TX.

I am honored and proud to have had Andrew as a student. His attitude, his hard work, and commitment helped him achieve success and discover his purpose in life.

If you reflect back on your life and others, you will see the seeds of attitudes being planted into our aspirations and then the thrill of watching success being manifested.

Always take time out of your busy schedule so that you can reflect on the positives. It will brighten up your day and make your life more rewarding.

Looking back, I can remember the time when our school voted for me to receive the teacher of the year award. I never thought that I would have a chance of receiving it, because we had lots of smart, experienced teachers with exceptional backgrounds, but the school selected me. When Ms. Sandoval, the principal told me the news, I was amazed and overwhelmed with joy.

I thought to myself, "How could someone like me receive such an honor?" But as I reflected back, I think that the students and staff members were moved by my attitude. I was told by staff members and students that everyone loved my attitude. A positive attitude can change your environment. It can bring a positive light into a negative situation. I believe that a positive attitude can change your world and make your life more interesting. Your attitude determines your level of success. If you develop a positive attitude, you will see the word as a blank canvas that's waiting for you, the artist to create a masterpiece.